Carnegie-Mellon University Press
Distributed by Columbia University Press
New York — Guilford, Surrey

©1980 Carnegie-Mellon University
Library of Congress Catalog Card Number 81-65946
ISBN Number 0-915604-49-3

The 1980 Benjamin F. Fairless Memorial Lectures

Douglas A. Fraser
& Fletcher L. Byrom

Failing Industries

The
Role
of
Government

Benjamin Fairless was president of United States Steel Corporation for fifteen years, and chairman of the board from 1952 until his retirement in 1955. A friend of Carnegie-Mellon University for many years, he served on the board of trustees from 1952 until his death. In 1959 he was named honorary chairman of the board.

Mr. Fairless died January 1, 1962.

The Benjamin F. Fairless Memorial Lectures endowment fund was established at Carnegie-Mellon University by friends of Mr. Fairless to support an annual series of lectures. Internationally known figures from the world of business, government, or education are invited each year to lecture at Carnegie-Mellon under the auspices of its Graduate School of Industrial Administration. In general, the lectures are concerned with some aspects of business or public administration; the relationships between business and government, management and labor; or a subject related to the themes of preserving economic freedom, human liberty, and the strengthening of individual enterprise — all of which were matters of deep concern to Mr. Fairless throughout his career.

The lectures in this volume were presented at Carnegie-Mellon University on November 11, 1980.

UAW President **Douglas A. Fraser** joined the automobile industry at the age of 18 when he went to work in the DeSoto plant of Chrysler Corporation.

He became active in Detroit's UAW Local 227 and was elected to various offices, including steward, chief steward, recording secretary and, finally, local president in 1943. He served three terms in that position.

In 1947 he was appointed an international representative and four years later became UAW President Walter P. Reuther's administrative assistant. In 1959 he was elected co-director of Region 1A.

In 1962, convention delegates elected him to the union's International Executive Board as a member-at-large and reelected him to that position in 1964, 1966, and 1968.

Mr. Fraser was elected a vice president at the union's 1970 convention, and president at the 1977 convention.

He is a member of the board of directors of the Chrysler Corporation, the first labor representative to be on the board of a U.S. corporation.

Mr. Fraser is an officer or member of numerous civic and governmental bodies and a member of the board of directors of various organizations, including the Full Employment Action Council, the NAACP, the National Housing Conference, the National Urban Coalition, New Detroit and the Economic Club of Detroit.

Fletcher L. Byrom joined Koppers Company in 1947 and held a variety of production, marketing and operating responsibilities before becoming general manager in 1958 of what is now the Organic Materials Group. He was elected president of the company and became a member of the board of directors in 1960. In 1967, he was named chief executive officer and became chairman of the board in 1970.

Mr. Byrom is chairman of the Committee for Economic Development and is a member of the Business Council and the Business Round Table. He is also a director of Catalyst. He was chairman of the Conference Board from 1974 to 1976.

He is on the board of directors of The Continental Group, Ralston Purina Company, Mellon Bank N.A., North American Philips Corporation, ASARCO, Richmond Tank Car Company, and the Advisory Board of Chemical Bank and Unilever, Ltd.

Failing Industries: The Role of Government

By Douglas A. Fraser

Re-industrialization is a term very much in vogue these days. Without a doubt, the debate over industrial policy has become a key economic issue of the 1980s. Yet despite broad agreement that many of our nation's basic manufacturing industries are in crisis, there is no consensus about what, if anything, should be done.

As I listen to and participate in this debate I partly feel vindicated — and increasingly discouraged. Vindicated, because we in the UAW have been talking about the need for economic planning in this country, and the need for more "economic democracy," for a very long time. Discouraged, because it took a crisis of such enormous magnitude — with devastating consequences for hundreds of thousands of workers, and whole regions of the country — to even get these issues before the public; and *still* there is little sign of forward momentum toward development and implementation of the kinds of policies that could really help. Instead of serious thinking about coherent approaches, we are witnessing an all-too-familiar spectacle: empty political debate over how far we should permit the hands of the clock to be rolled back; a Congress so captive of competing special interests that it seems incapable of any significant legislative progress; and within the Executive branch, fierce inter-agency rivalry to carve up the industrial policy "ox," with little regard for the public interest. Corporate America is lining up for the choice cuts; my fear is that no matter how the ox gets carved up, the workers will be gored.

The fact is, there *is* no coherent industrial policy in this country; nor has any yet been seriously considered. We do need one badly. Further across the board tax concessions and relaxation of governmental regulations, as many corporations are proposing, are not the answer. It is ironic that conservatives who criticize government for "throwing money" at social problems appear to advocate exactly that when it comes to industrial policy and the recipients are corporations. According to their view, it is a waste of taxpayers' dollars for government to ease the plight of the aging, the poor, and the unemployed, by means of programs which are alleged to be unplanned, untargeted and uncontrolled. Yet that is precisely the kind of industrial non-policy demanded by corporate America.

Failing Industries — Or A Failing Economy?

In addressing the question of failing industries, we must keep in mind that we are talking about real people — workers and their families — who are affected. Too often, policymakers tend to focus on the corporation as an entity and ignore the workers that are to suffer real devastation as the result of a business failure. We in the UAW, for example, fought for the Chrysler loan guarantee legislation not to "bail out" the Chrysler Corporation. We fought to save the jobs of the Chrysler workers and the jobs of thousands of workers in supplier companies that do business with Chrysler.

In my judgment, our nation's problem is not "failing industries." Rather, it is a failing *economy*. If good jobs — for which retraining and relocation assistance were guaranteed — were plentiful in all regions of our country, would industrial workers cling desperately to their present employment in a "failing industry?" If there was a comprehensive system of national health insurance in this country — that dispensed decent medical care to all as a matter of right — would workers trapped in a "failing industry" feel so desperate when job loss causes termination of their union-negotiated, employer-paid medical insurance? If the Social Security system provided every retired and disabled American with a decent and adequate standard of living, would the prospect of pension loss by older workers permanently displaced from a "failing industry" be anywhere near as grim? It is the manifest failure of our economic system in these and so many other areas to provide decent jobs and economic security to millions of our people that makes the failure of a basic industry such a serious and far-reaching problem. If our economic "engine" were healthy, generating a high and rising standard of living for all, producing wealth in abundance and distributing it fairly, then I doubt that there would be any problem of "failing industries." Displaced workers would not fear for their futures, and would not suffer devastating economic — and personal — loss. Communities and entire regions would not be threatened with wholesale devastation, or long-term economic decline.

The reality is different. Workers trapped in a "failing industry" do face enormous personal loss. For them, and for members of their families, job loss is a wrenching emotional experience. It causes deep scars which often never heal. Workers who lose their jobs in a "failing industry" — which often means a failing local economy — may go months or even years before they find another. If they do find a new job, it is likely to pay far less than the one they lost, be even less secure, and have worse working conditions. Even obtaining an inferior job may require uprooting one's family, leaving old friends, and relocating hundreds of miles away. Valued skills acquired during a lifetime of work in a "failing industry" may be virtually untransferable to the new industry or occupation. For a worker whose career has been spent in industrial employment, the transition to a new job in the supposedly ascendant service or "tertiary" sector of the economy is far from smooth. For minority workers abandoned in declining central cities, that transition may be all but impossible. Older workers, and workers whose health is poor — even though they were able to perform their prior jobs perfectly well — are in an especially difficult position when thrust into the unemployment lines after being displaced from a "failing industry."

While unemployed, workers are stripped of medical insurance coverage at precisely the worst time, when their health and the health of their families is most at risk. Fewer than a third of the unemployed in this country have any medical insurance at all. Those who do are forced to pay exorbitant premiums, on an individual rather than group rate, out of unemployment checks which amount, on average, to less than half their prior pay. Not only does our unemployment compensation system have the lowest income replacement ratio and duration of coverage in the industrialized world, there is also no other industrialized country which does not provide basic medical insurance coverage for its unemployed.

Despite ERISA protection, current and future retirees who have spent their work careers in a "failing industry" often face substantial losses in retirement income, compared with workers whose industries are robust. Early retirement supplements and recently negotiated increases in benefit levels can suddenly be stripped away; it does not take many years of double-digit inflation to erode the purchasing power of pension benefits which are frozen permanently at five year old levels. As the ratio of active workers to retirees in a "failing industry" — or company — inexorably declines, we in the labor movement are faced with an increasingly grim tradeoff in collective bargaining, between meeting the legitimate and pressing needs of our active members, and the equally legitimate and pressing needs of our retirees.

The joys of homeownership can become a trap and a curse for

workers displaced from a "failing industry" in a one-industry town.

If the impact on workers who become victims of an industry's decline was purely economic, that would be bad enough, but the reality is even worse. Although they are not talked about much, the damaging health and psychological consequences of job loss are — or should be — widely known. Using national data for the period 1940-1973, Prof. Harvey Brenner of Johns Hopkins University found that unemployment plays a statistically significant role in affecting several forms of "social trauma." In particular, he concludes that a one percent increase in the aggregate unemployment rate sustained over a period of six years has been associated with approximately:

— 37,000 total deaths (including 20,000 cardiovascular deaths)
— 920 suicides
— 650 homicides
— 500 deaths from cirrhosis of the liver
— 4,000 state mental hospital admissions
— 3,300 state prison admissions

These results, of course, do not speak directly to the question of unemployment resulting from displacement of workers from "failing industry," but one would suspect that permanent layoffs cause even more "social trauma" than unemployment arising from other causes. We know, for example, that in the aftermath of the Federal Mogul Corporation's closing of its roller bearing plant in Detroit, eight of the nearly 2,000 affected workers took their own lives.

Dimensions and Magnitude of the Current Crisis

For me and the membership of the UAW, these grim statistics are cause for the gravest possible concern. It is no secret that auto workers are in the throes of the worst economic crisis since the Great Depression. Unemployment rates have reached depression levels in much of the industrial Midwest. In Detroit, the unemployment rate reached 18.3 percent. It has not been higher since the Great Depression, even at the trough of the last severe auto slump in 1975. The unemployment rate in certain other towns is even worse. In Pontiac, it has reached 24.3 percent. In Flint, Michigan — home of the famous Sitdown Strikes that gave birth to the UAW — 23 percent are out of work. In Saginaw, the figure is 19.3

percent. The Indiana towns of Anderson and Kokomo have unemployment rates of 22 percent and 20.1 percent, respectively.

During the second week of November — more than a year and a half after the current auto slump began — over 180,000 auto workers at General Motors, American Motors, Chrysler and Ford were on indefinite layoff. Thousands have exhausted all benefits, including unemployment compensation, collectively bargained supplemental unemployment benefits, and TRA. Including supplier companies, the Department of Transportation has estimated total auto slump-related job loss at around 700,000. Many supplier workers have long since been forced onto the relief rolls, having never been covered by supplemental unemployment benefit plans. Nor, due to a cruel inequity in TRA, are the supplier industry workers eligible for benefits under that program.

In addition to the massive unemployment caused by the auto slump, the impact on city finances and services has been devastating. To take just one example, Detroit's fiscal crisis is currently forcing the layoff of some 1,100 police, at a time when crime in that city, as a direct result of the unemployment crisis, is once again on the rise, after several years of decline. Worse yet, the police layoffs will have a serious effect on an affirmative action program that is essential to preserve the effectiveness of law enforcement and prevent further unraveling of the social fabric. City services, already pared to the bone, face further cutbacks. A similar situation prevails in all of the other previously-mentioned cities, and many other cities as well.

At the state level in Michigan, finances are so strapped that the governor has made a shocking proposal to slash the welfare rolls — at a time when welfare is the only remaining source of income for thousands of unfortunate workers.

Of course, this is not the first cyclical downturn in the auto industry — far from it, despite the unprecedented length and severity of the current slump. What is new and especially disturbing about the current crisis is the unprecedented number of plant closings and *permanent* job cutbacks, in contrast to the *cyclical* unemployment of past crises. In the last year roughly, the Chrysler Corporation alone has permanently closed its Lyons Trim plant (Lyons, Michigan); the Fostoria Foundry (Fostoria, Ohio); Hamtramck Assembly (Hamtramck, Michigan); Windsor Engine (Windsor, Ontario); Missouri Truck (Fenton, Missouri); and Eight Mile-Outer Drive Stamping (Detroit). The Huber Foundry (also Detroit) is scheduled to permanently close later this month.

Other Chrysler closings and permanent cutbacks are widely expected.

Ford and General Motors have also announced major permanent closings or relocations in the last year, with more announcements probably in store. Among the suppliers, including such large and prosperous firms as Dana and Ex-Cell-O, there has been an epidemic of permanent closings and relocations. Already as of May, at least 90 supplier plants were known to have closed during the current crisis, including both UAW and non-UAW plants. By now, that figure is substantially higher.

Is Auto A "Failing Industry?"

Given the dimensions and magnitude of the present crisis — including its structural character in contrast with past cyclical crises, the unprecedented loss in market share of North American producers to foreign and especially Japanese competitors, and the particular severity of the problems afflicting two of the Big Three auto corporations — it would be easy to conclude that the North American auto industry is indeed a "failing industry." That conclusion would be premature. The resources and resourcefulness of the auto industry should not be underestimated. Comparisons and parallels drawn with other industries which more clearly are in decline are misleading and wrong.

Some argue that the present crisis stems from the failure of the North American auto industry to make a product which suits consumers' needs, at a price they can afford, and of a quality which they have come to expect. Though oversimplified — and though this explanation overlooks the impact of the aggressive and injurious competition of the Japanese auto industry — there is a kernel of truth in these popular perceptions. The UAW has, I am proud to say, leveled our share of criticism at the industry for these and other shortcomings down through the years. For it is the workers who suffer the most from the bad decisions and wrong priorities of corporate management. The present danger is that a cynical public is not ready to believe that the industry has really come to grips with these past shortcomings — that it has come up with the products people need, or that quality has properly been elevated to a much higher corporate priority than in the past. Such cynicism would be entirely understandable; yet if it prevails it will again be the workers who suffer.

How did we get where we are? A bygone era of cheap gas, subsidized highways and cheap FHA mortgages gave rise to a U.S.

car market which historically has been very different from the world outside North America. In the U.S., the companies emphasized large cars, and spent huge sums on styling changes. Every now and then, a smaller new "economy model" would be introduced; but inevitably within a few years, that model had sprouted tail fins, increased greatly in weight, and dropped way down in gas mileage. Design, engineering and manufacturing competence with respect to small cars was never really developed; cheap gas, "wide-open spaces" and an overriding desire for personal luxury and comfort meant that the American new car buyer wasn't interested. Small car capability was left for the companies' European subsidiaries.

Quality, reliability and durability of product did not seem that important to a "throw-away" society which institutionalized waste and even glorified it. In that atmosphere, it became easy for management to sacrifice quality in their push for production. The industry put its emphasis on quantity, rather than quality — an orientation that can and has already begun to change.

This bygone era produced some remarkable prosperity and profits for the auto industry. The workers suffered periodic bouts of cyclical unemployment, but when they were working our members enjoyed the benefits of steady progress in wages, benefits and paid time off won by our union down through the years. Moreover, the pioneering SUB program we were able to negotiate provided an important cushion during the inevitable periods of unemployment. These gains for our members were more than paid for by increases in auto industry productivity, which rose rapidly during the post-World War II period, far outstripping the gains recorded in other sectors of the economy.

In the early 1970s, the Congress began to attempt instilling a degree of foresight and vision into the industry's planning, with the goal of protecting the public's vital interest in availability of fuel-efficient, safer and less-polluting cars. The industry complained bitterly, and fought these early and subsequent regulatory attempts tooth and nail. Their information monopoly concerning feasibility and cost of proposed regulations was exploited to maximum advantage in the short-run; but this only bred suspicion and hostility on the part of the regulators and the public.

The Japanese government and auto industry, meanwhile, was following a well-laid plan to achieve manufacturing competence and eventual competitive dominance on a global scale. They emphasized manufacturing technology, and product simplicity and quality. Their achievements have been widely mythologized. (Contrary to widespread press reports, including in *Ward's Automotive Reports*, the Japanese do *not* have an assembly plant with 67 workers turning out 1500 cars per day. They have, however, become formidable competitors.)

Looking back, it is hard to believe that from 1975 through the winter of 1979, the American public moved away from smaller cars, as the price of gasoline remained relatively stable compared with other prices and memories of gas lines faded. The abrupt reappearance of gasoline lines, triggered by the temporary disruption of supply in the wake of the Iranian revolution, and soaring gas prices as a result of deregulation of oil prices and continued OPEC price increases, brought a sudden end to this lapse into pre-1973 reverie. Had it not been for the fuel economy regulations promulgated by the federal government — which the UAW supported — the ensuing crisis would have been even worse.

In the months that followed, the U.S. market was deluged by a veritable flood of imported cars, especially from Japan. The U.S. industry was unable to meet the rapid and abrupt shift in car buyers' preferences; Japanese auto companies were poised and ready to capitalize on this sudden advantage. Imports skyrocketed to a 27.5% share of the U.S. market during early 1980, compared with 15.5% for 1978. Of this unprecedented 27.5% import share, Japanese-made vehicles accounted for the overwhelming proportion — nearly 23% of the total U.S. market. Massive unemployment in this country has been the result, while auto plants in Japan added extra shifts and worked heavy overtime to build vehicles for export to the U.S.

The crisis was further compounded by the economic recession, triggered in part by the import-related slump in U.S. car sales, and in part by a misguided and tragic attempt to wring inflation out of the economy by tightening credit. The recession caused further steep declines in domestic auto production and employment.

No matter how strong the recovery from the present deep slump, an awful lot of plants — which have been permanently closed — will not be recalling any workers. We are extremely fearful that we are witnessing — perhaps for the first time in the U.S. auto industry's history — massive, structural, permanent dislocation. The long-lasting consequences for countless thousands of workers and dozens of communities could be horrendous.

Therefore, while we expect that with the right government policies, the industry will make a satisfactory recovery from the onslaught of Japanese vehicles and the many other problems which beset it, the sad truth is that the industry's recovery is not going to help all of those workers and communities. The very steps which the industry will be taking to reestablish its profitability and international competitive position will cause further permanent dislocations. For the auto worker, the recent past has been characterized by grim retrenchment; while what the future holds in store is painful restructuring.

That restructuring will entail massive changes in both product and process, at a capital cost estimated at $80 billion by the Big Four alone over the next five years. The industry that emerges may be radically different from the industry today. We already know that cars will be far smaller and lighter. This could involve massive changes in sourcing: cars will have a lot less iron and steel, and a lot more aluminum, plastics and electronic components. The dawn of the "world car" may bring an internationalization of production on a hitherto unknown scale, with uncertain but possibly major impact on the job security of American workers. How many more plants — not only in the auto industry — will be permanently closed, as car makers substitute plastic for steel, and industrial robots for live labor, in the years ahead? We in the UAW have always welcomed new technology and the higher productivity it brings. Yet as new technology impacts on the workplace, we must give priority to its impact on workers. Shorter work time to spread available employment and use of attrition rather than layoff are approaches that must be explored.

A recent survey of auto industry and supplier executives by the firm of Arthur Andersen found that much of the industry's planned capital spending will go for new plants. The survey also makes clear that the industry will be looking increasingly outside its traditional geographic home for new plant construction, particularly among suppliers. Thus there is little reason to be confident that increased capacity of plastics, light metal, and electronic automotive suppliers will be sited within commuting range of existing supplier capacity which will cut back. The same Arthur Andersen study concludes that foreign sourcing will increase, as will corporate runaways and relocations to avoid unions and to obtain lower wage labor.

In auto assembly, other analysts have predicted that, with anticipated strides in productivity, annual capacity of a typical new assembly plant will be sharply higher than the current level.

Given probable growth rates of auto production, there is reason to fear that there will be more assembly plant closings than new openings in the years ahead. Nor is there any guarantee that the new plants which are built will be located in areas accessible to workers from the old plants being closed. Without public policy that encourages and facilitates planning for *people* as well as profits, the implications of these developments point to rough sledding for our union and its members.

Corporate Prescription to Cut Regulations and Business Taxes is the Wrong Medicine

With respect to the nature of its product, few industries have been more affected by "government regulations" than the auto industry. The past decade has witnessed major federal legislation in the areas of fuel economy, emissions, and safety, which have had profound consequences for the industry. The public has benefited greatly from these regulations; nor have they been all bad from the standpoint of the industry. As Henry Ford candidly admitted, fuel economy standards were a critical factor in stimulating development of small car productive capacity. Particularly revealing is the fact that General Motors treats mandatory fuel economy increases as "product improvements," rather than regulatory costs. Well over three-fifths of total auto industry regulatory "costs" are associated with fuel economy improvements.

In the areas of auto emissions and safety, moreover, federal regulations have been extremely beneficial to the public. Air quality improvements, and improved auto safety, represent significant gains in our collective "quality of life." It is true that the burden of meeting these regulatory standards falls most heavily on the smaller producers — more heavily on Chrysler than on Ford, and more heavily on Ford than on General Motors. The appropriate solution is to help the smaller companies meet the standards, not to relax the standards. This need not involve any cost to the public. An important example is the lifting of anti-trust restrictions on the exchange of emissions control technology between auto companies.

More generally, the present campaign against beneficial governmental regulations is dishonest and wrong. The notion that all regulations are costly and inflationary is a phony argument which ignores the social benefits that result from regulations. What the critics overlook is that health, safety, environmental, pure food and drug, and other regulations are there for a reason — in most cases, to protect the public against a litany of outrageous corporate abuses. Typically, the abuses went on for years before regulatory action was taken. It is no accident that the agencies which have recently been most active and effective in discharging their mandate, such as OSHA, have borne the brunt of the corporate anti-regulatory attack. Testimony to the effectiveness of OSHA is the fact that the occupational injury rate has tended to decline in recent years, reversing a ten year climb prior to enactment of the OSHA Act. With respect to the far more serious problem of occupational *disease*, much work remains but important progress has been made. All of this has been costly to corporations; apparently too many of them would rather be free to poison and maim their workers. As a result, OSHA has come under heavy corporate attack. During the last session of Congress, some 50 separate bills were introduced to weaken OSHA. The most serious of these, Sen. R. Schweiker's (R-Pa.) euphemistically titled "OSHA Improvement Act," would have exempted 90 percent of all workplaces from OSHA's jurisdiction. Workers would no longer be able to obtain an OSHA inspection by filing a complaint. OSHA would lose authority to initiate inspections except in the event of a workplace fatality and a few other instances. The bill also would establish a mechanism for corporations to avoid potential liability for OSHA fines altogether.

No matter how serious the abuse, corporations have *rarely* voluntarily "policed" their own actions with any consistency or success, yet they have consistently opposed any public attempt to achieve that goal. What kind of social jungle would we be living in today if we relied on corporate "voluntarism" to protect investors against stock market fraud, to protect workers' rights to organize, to protect the quality of the environment, and to protect the civil rights of women and minorities? There are, without question, "socially responsible" corporations which try to adhere to decent standards. However, in the long run — unless there is legislation which subjects everybody to the same rules — a "socially responsible" corporation faces an insurmountable disadvantage compared with its more greedy competitors. Perhaps Keynes put it best, when he said that "capitalism is the extraordinary belief that the nastiest of men for the nastiest of motives, will somehow work for the benefit of us all." If that respected economist is too radical for you, let me quote Adam Smith, who described businessmen of his day as "an order of men whose interest is never exactly the same as the public, who have generally an interest to deceive and even to oppress the public, and who accordingly, upon many occasions, both deceived and oppressed it." You do not have to be a great economist or moral philospher to know that when it comes to protecting the public against corporate abuse, government regulations are necessary; "voluntarism" will not work.

As to the second principal element of the corporate program, further federal tax concessions — it is difficult to accept those relief proposals as they currently are structured. There can be no question that there is the need for massive amounts of capital to facilitate the modernization of our plants and equipment. The key, however, is to design capital formation mechanisms that make possible that modernization without encouraging irresponsible and unacceptable results. Tax policy should not, for example, result in corporations abandoning urban areas and high unemployment regions. Instead, we need a tax program that actively encourages "targeted" investment in such areas. Across-the-board tax breaks, as some propose, must be rejected in favor of tax policy that spurs reindustrialization in a socially responsible way.

Other elements of the corporate reindustrialization agenda appear to include inequitable wage restraint for working people despite raging inflation without comparable restraints on profits and other non-wage forms of income; and general public sacrifice and "belt-tightening" via reduced government spending on needed social programs.

Some sectors of corporate America appear to expect labor to cheerfully swallow this distasteful brew. In spite of the onesidedness of their program, the need to revitalize failing industry spawns talk of cooperation between labor and management. That cooperation can be crucial in saving workers' jobs and in rebuilding American industry.

Yet it becomes extremely difficult for workers to understand why cooperation occurs when some in the business community aggressively oppose the right of labor unions to even exist. Unfortunately, these irresponsible elements continue to wage a direct campaign against the legitimacy of the labor movement at the very time when we do need to be working together to get our economy moving again.

Instead of blaming taxes, government regulations and their workers, it is high time for corporate America to shoulder its fair share of the blame for the shape that our basic industries are in. Too often, profitable corporations in certain of these industries failed to reinvest in new plants and equipment and paid out huge dividends or bought out existing businesses instead. In this regard, the steel industry has been a notable offender.

In the U.S., investment financed largely out of retained corporate earnings has in recent years amounted to less than 10 percent of GNP, compared with 21 percent for Japan and 14 percent for West Germany. Yet corporate profits and returns on investment do not appear to be any higher in these countries. With respect to research and development, in 1964 2.1 percent of our GNP was devoted to this vital function, while in 1979, the proportion was only 1.7 percent. Strategies of corporate executives in this country all too often focus on the short-term goal of profit maximization today, rather than on doing what is necessary for stable employment — and even profits — over the long haul. A successful reindustrialization program must include this badly needed reorientation of corporate priorities.

What is the Proper Role of Government?

As I have indicated, industry is already taking the steps to assure access to whatever federal assistance will be necessary to insure its survival. In that process, they have already received and undoubtedly will continue to receive various forms of government assistance. But what about the workers? What is desperately needed is some assurance that workers will not become the unassisted victims of industry's restructuring. Preliminary indications, based on my initial experience as a member of President Carter's Auto Industry Advisory Committee, do not provide much cause for optimism that industry understands or appreciates the needs and concerns of their workers in the current crisis. Executives of the industry initially would not even agree with my suggestion that plant closings and economic dislocations should be considered as part of the agenda of the committee, though ultimately — with the Secretary of Transportation's backing — this critical topic did get adopted as an agenda item.

People do have a legitimate right to expect a reasonable amount of economic certainty and security in their lives. Achievement of these aims for working people and the less privileged members of society has long been a priority goal of the labor movement. This means, in the present context, that we believe it is the job of government to see to it that workers who would become victims of industry's necessary restructuring are not simply forgotten. They must be "made whole." The government can either do this directly, or it can set standards of conduct for industry. If, as economists are fond of arguing, "capital mobility" confers benefits on society as a whole, then it is only reasonable and fair that those who would become the victims of that mobility should be properly assisted in shouldering the burden of adjustment. What is often all too conveniently overlooked is that capital mobility has its costs as well as its rewards; there is presently no systematic public procedure for assuring equity in the distribution of these costs and rewards. If a company pollutes a river, it is widely accepted that some obligation is owed to the injured fishermen downstream. Is there not a comparable obligation to long-service workers who are prematurely relegated to the scrapheap as a result of a profit-maximizing decision by their former employer to withdraw capital from a "declining" industry and invest it in another?

Beyond assuring equity and fairness, it is the responsibility of government to overcome the notorious short-sightedness of U.S. industry and its single-minded emphasis on short-run profit maximization. Since industry will not and indeed cannot voluntarily adopt a longer-term perspective, government — in the public interest — must participate in the development of the nation's long term industrial strategy. It is essential to provide public input into major private investment and disinvestment decisions to protect the public interest. If freedom is really to be preserved in this country, it is critical that we find a way to make corporate decision-making, with respect to this issue and other key issues, more accountable and democratic.

The focus of the government's efforts with respect to "failing industries" should be job retention and creation; income maintenance and social insurance protection are also important. This does not mean susidizing workers to remain in unproductive, outmoded occupations. Just because an industry may be in decline does not mean that its workers, plant and equipment could not be highly productive if systematically converted to alternative uses.

Many of the auto supplier plants which have been closed are part of large, profitable, diversified corporations which at the time of a closing knew full well that they would be opening a new plant in a different product line very soon. With proper planning and foresight, there is no reason why the new non-auto plants could not be built near the old plants which are to be closed, to provide jobs, with retraining if necessary, to the auto workers who will be displaced. In fact, many of the existing plants could be refurbished to produce the new product line.

There can be a systematic, public process for identifying unmet current and future needs — either of a non-market nature or to which the "market" is responding too slowly. And those unmet needs can be matched in a systematic way with the workers and the factories which are slated to close. Some experts have proposed that auto workers, plants and equipment could be readily re-utilized for production of oil and gas drilling and exploration equipment, or industrial co-generation equipment. That would truly be a humane and rational use of our nation's resources — to plan a smooth conversion of that part of our industrial economy most hurt by the energy crisis to products that are desperately needed to mitigate that crisis. The U.S. Synfuels Corp., a quasi-public entity, will be dispensing billions of dollars to foster development of alternative energy sources in the years ahead. Given the foresight and the political will, this spending could be targeted to provide new economic hope to unemployed workers and devastated industrial communities throughout our nation.

In the short run, if loss of market to foreign competitors is the cause of an industry's failure, temporary import relief may be justified. In the auto industry, the case for temporary import relief is very strong. As the only wide-open auto market in the world, the U.S. has become the "residual market" for imported vehicles — which means unemployment automatically gets exported to us. Briefly, the scenario is this: Japan "targets" its auto industry for vigorous growth; Europe and other parts of the world, anxious to protect their domestic employment, keep Japanese imports out; those imports get diverted to us.

In a similar way, Mexico imposes strict local content requirements on its auto industry. This leads Chrysler and Ford to shift plans and build critical new four cylinder engine capacity in Mexico; meanwhile, hundreds of thousands of auto workers in the U.S. are unemployed. I harbor no grudge against Mexico, which is a developing country that badly wants to industrialize — but what about the auto workers in the U.S. who become unemployed? Clearly it is the function of government to protect American workers against actions by other governments which deprive us of our jobs. In the UAW we have long believed and continue to believe in the principle of free trade, as long as it is *fair* trade.

Government cannot stand idly by in the face of injurious trade practices which carry grave risk of causing permanent damage to an industry as basic and important to our economy as auto. It must assure breathing room while the domestic industry retools to meet the competitive challenge.

But policies to mitigate the sharp drop in auto sales are by no means enough. Jobs must be found for the thousands of workers who may not be called back, even after sales recover. Workers who become victims of the industry's restructuring must be protected. Communities whose economic base is in jeopardy as a result of that restructuring must have their economic vitality restored.

It is the role of government to make sure that these valid and critically important goals are achieved. This means that government must set and enforce standards of industry behavior. And it means that corporations must abandon certain knee-jerk reactions to automatically oppose government intervention. The legitimacy of a governmental role can be seen in the auto industry in recent months. Certainly Chrysler Corporation had to abandon old philosophical hangups as it actively sought government intervention to save the company from failure. Likewise, Ford Motor Company joined the UAW's effort for government action to restrain the flood of foreign imports into this country.

Government also must act as entrepreneur in the *public* interest, to weigh and evaluate the social consequences of private investment and disinvestment decisions. In these respects, the United States lags far behind much of the rest of the industrialized world. The "industrial Darwinism" of the United States contrasts markedly with Western Europe's more humane and farsighted approach, which recognizes and forces business to take account of the human and social consequences of their retrenchment and restructuring decisions. We have needlessly become the victims of our national failure to protect and to plan.

Let me reiterate that this is not an argument for perpetual subsidy to inefficient firms or truly declining industries. The debate over whether to help ailing industries restructure, or to promote new industries in their place, misses the point; the challenge to government — and its clear responsibility — is to devise and enforce public policies which assure that the emerging new industries actually absorb the workers who will be cast off by the industries in decline, in such a way that those workers feel personally assured that they will make a relatively smooth transition.

We are very far from achieving that goal in this country. Even the tentative first step of requiring a departing employer to give advance notice is meeting with a strenuous corporate attack. Advance notice is vital; how can we plan effectively to assist victims of dislocation without it? Even Peter Drucker, no ally of labor, has advised corporate America to reform voluntarily or face plant closing legislation. Even the *Wall Street Journal*, which has likened that proposed legislation to the Soviet exit tax, admits that corporations do owe an obligation to departed workers and communities. Virtually every other industrialized country recognizes this obligation by law. Our own government claims to support guidelines for multinational corporations, adopted in 1976 by the OECD, which provide that:

> In considering changes in their operations which would have major effects upon the livelihood of their employees, in particular in the case of the closure of an entity involving collective lay-offs or dismissals, (enterprises should) provide reasonable notice of such changes to representatives of their employees, and where appropriate to the relevant governmental authorities, and co-operate with the employee representatives and appropriate governmental authorities so as to mitigate to the maximum extent practicable adverse effects.

For American workers, implementation of this guideline remains an unfulfilled promise.

Some of the closings and relocations which are occurring under the smokescreen of the current retrenchment — however much they may enhance a corporation's bottom line — are imposing horrendous costs on the rest of society. In certain of these cases, if the social costs were properly factored into the decision-making process, an alternative to the shutdown would be found. To prevent such closings is the job of government. To do that job effectively requires legislation.

Many other closings and relocations are necessary and valid, from a social point of view. But it is the job of government to make sure that such closings cause the least possible harm to affected workers and communities, whom departing employers must be forced by law to treat fairly and decently. For thousands of workers and numerous communities that have become victims of the current retrenchment in auto and other industries, it may already be too late. This need not be true of the restructuring which lies ahead.

Do we really lack the foresight and vision in this country, to plan for full and productive utilization of our nation's resources? That is tragic, if it's true. And it is by no means *inevitable*.

Presently in the United States, corporate decisions to close or move a plant are often made and carried out in a way that can only be called inhumane. Corporations planning a shutdown or relocation in too many cases go out of their way to mislead their workers and the community where the plant is located. These irresponsible companies are experts at sowing deception as to their true intentions. One all-too-common practice is to "milk" a once-viable plant, using profits to finance runaway expansion, acquisitions, or diversification to other product lines at distant locations. Corporations desiring an orderly phaseout of production often deny until the last possible minute their intent to close or move, even though plans to close were probably made months or years earlier. At university-sponsored management seminars, corporate shutdown planners are advised to extend the veil of secrecy even within corporate management as far as possible, except for individuals with a clear "need to know."

When the closure is finally about to occur, the corporation engages in "surface bargaining" with its union, if there is one. The best we can usually do for our members in such situations is to win a certain amount of severance pay, fringe benefit continuation, and retirement income protection. Transfer rights, unless already provided in the pre-existing collective bargaining agreement, are usually out of the question. Corporations which close or move a plant are extremely reluctant to grant even "preferential hiring rights" to former employees unless they are required to do so by the existing contract. Workers from a closed plant can even find themselves blacklisted, unable to obtain work in their local community.

Perhaps most reprehensible of all are plant closures which result from corporate decisions to "socialize" the costs associated with an aging workforce. In such cases, unrestricted corporate freedom to close and move plants can be cynically used to undermine the protection of older workers which the seniority system was intended to provide. We have found, for example, that no sooner do we negotiate a new early retirement program, than a company may close a plant shortly before large numbers of workers would become eligible to receive benefits thereunder. This was tried recently by one large and highly profitable auto supplier, whose plant employing over 1,000 UAW members is about to be permanently closed. That same corporation, ironically, announced at about the same time that it would diversify into non-automotive products, in part by reconverting an abandoned textile plant of another corporation, thousands of miles away, to home water heater production. Needless to say, the company has no plans to reconvert the auto supplier plant it is closing down.

The pattern we have observed is almost unbelievably shocking: hundreds or even thousands of loyal, long-service workers unceremoniously dumped on short or no notice, after being fed systematic "disinformation," denied transfer rights and even preferential hiring consideration, given no opportunities for retraining or assistance in job placement, possibly "blacklisted" by other local employers on account of their age or union activism, and stripped of medical insurance, life insurance and the chance to retire with dignity. The corporation which has profited from its workers' labor down through the years has virtually no obligations. It reaps only the rewards from an astute, albeit cynical, business decision. That decision, in all likelihood, was doubtless made even more lucrative by all manner of tax incentives and other public subsidies.

As somebody once said of Royal Little, the conglomerateur who founded the modern Textron by buying old plants cheap, milking them to finance other acquisitions, then closing them down: "I don't know whether Mr. Little has broken any laws. But if not, the laws should be changed."

Beyond curbing the aforementioned kinds of abuses, an appropriate public reindustrialization strategy must be based on the principle that it is not enough to assist industry in its necessary restructuring. Workers and communities who become the victims of that restructuring must also be assisted.

Is Chrysler a Model?

Given the attention which has been focused on that corporation, many are asking whether a "model" for U.S. industrial policy is the kind of federal assistance that has been rendered to Chrysler under the Loan Guarantee Act. In my view, that is not the case. While what was done to assist Chrysler was necessary and proper, in reality it was more a reflection of our nation's lack of a coherent, farsighted industrial policy than an example of what that policy should be.

Even as an urgently needed "ad hoc" measure, the federal loan guarantee approach differed substantially from what we had initially proposed. The UAW advocated a direct equity investment in Chrysler by the federal government, based on the notion that if public capital is at risk, there should be a corresponding degree of public ownership and control. I am fully aware that public ownership, particularly of an enterprise in trouble, is no panacea; but this mechanism would have enhanced the potential for imaginative stewardship of the corporation in the public interest. Presently, the Loan Guarantee Board — the federal "superboard" which will oversee the corporation until all guaranteed loans have been repaid — has as its overriding goal to assure that the guaranteed loans are in fact repaid. There has been no impetus from this oversight body to plan for "conversion" of idled Chrysler facilities and workers to alternative production. There has been no impetus from this body to use Chrysler as a kind of national "laboratory" for public development of safer, more fuel-efficient, less-polluting cars. This is not to criticize the dedicated cabinet officers who are members of the Loan Guarantee Board; rather, the problem lies in the limited scope of their legislative mandate and the narrow concept of public "stewardship" which that mandate entails.

Workers were singled out for sacrifice under the legislation in far greater measure, relative to their means, than any other "constituent group." Over the current three year contract period, a typical Chrysler worker fortunate enough to remain employed will permanently lose roughly $5,000 in wages, fringe benefits and paid time off compared with his UAW brother or sister doing precisely the same work at GM or Ford.

In spite of these and other drawbacks and limitations, the Loan Guarantee Act necessarily received our wholehearted support and endorsement, once it became clear that it was the only politically feasible way to save so many thousands of jobs. Our overriding interest was and continues to be worker protection, not survival of Chrysler as a corporate entity. Unfortunately, at the time only the latter was politically attainable, and even to attain this, the workers had to pay a very high price.

Even the form of assistance which was ultimately enacted met with widespread opposition. Critics charged that to assist Chrysler would be to tamper with the most basic precepts of the "free enterprise system," according to which only fit corporations deserve to survive. The fact that there was ample precedent for assisting Chrysler did little to assuage critics who did not like the precedents.

Helping Chrysler, in the critics' view, was like giving the losing team in an important baseball game an extra turn at bat. What the critics failed to realize was that this was no game; a Chrysler failure threatened to erase the livelihood of hundreds of thousands of workers and plunge dependent communities into deep and long-lasting depression. Opponents of assistance somehow managed to ignore the staggeringly high cost of *not* helping Chrysler. Just the tax loss to the public, coupled with transfer payments to the unemployed, alone amounted to a huge sum which dwarfed the probable cost of the guaranteed loans — which if repaid will actually yield considerable *income* to the Treasury.

Despite widespread misconceptions to the contrary, the terms of the Loan Guarantee Act were such that other financially troubled corporations will not be anxious to line up at the "trough." The terms exacted by Congress — quite properly — were tough and distasteful to the corporation.

The local and regional impacts, and impact on minority workers resulting from a shutdown, would have been devastating. Even the unlikely event that domestic car production rather than increased import penetration would have taken up the slack resulting from a Chrysler shutdown would have provided little help to unemployed Chrysler workers, given the numbers of GM and Ford workers already laid off who would first have had to be recalled, and the fact that few of their plants are nearby.

Bankruptcy was advocated by one vigorous Senate opponent of Chrysler assistance; yet it was widely agreed that liquidation rather than successful reorganization would have been the probable outcome of that cavalier recommendation.

The heavy regulatory burden imposed on Chrysler to meet federal emission and safety standards provided yet another justification for federal assistance.

Clearly, in spite of all the foregoing arguments, if — even given the proposed assistance — Chrysler did not have a reasonable chance to successfully restructure and survive, then the case for assistance would not have been as compelling. While some would say with respect to this question that the jury on Chrysler is still out, it is my belief that the prognosis for survival of the corporation, without need for further assistance beyond that already available to it, is very good.

What is in doubt, unfortunately, is the fate of thousands of workers and a number of Chrysler-dependent communities as the corporation restructures. The fact that so little has been done to assist these victims of the corporation's restructuring is a major disappointment. In the absence of federal loan guarantees, however, I am firmly convinced that a far worse catastrophe would have occurred.

In spite of the difficulties and disappointments, we have accomplished a number of things. During the extremely difficult collective bargaining which preceded enactment of the loan guarantee legislation, Chrysler agreed to nominate me as UAW representative to the corporation's board of directors. Though this may be no more than a small beginning, it is a pioneering step toward the vital goal of giving workers a meaningful voice in corporate decisions which critically affect them.

One tangible benefit is that, as a result of my suggestion, the corporation has established a board-level Plant and Human Resources Utilization Committee. The purpose of that committee is to consider ways and means of averting or cushioning the impact on workers who would otherwise be left out as the corporation restructures.

We are also tackling the vital issue of product quality in a new cooperative approach. Our union has taken on the firm obligation of policing management's duty to set and enforce the high standards of product quality which consumers today deserve and expect. We expect — and if it becomes necessary, we will force — management to provide a work environment that permits and encourages the highest standards of quality workmanship; and we will not shirk from our obligation to inform each and every one of our members that if management fulfills its part of this bargain, our members have a duty to fulfill theirs.

The real challenge — of providing meaningful assistance to the workers and communities who become victims of the restructuring of Chrysler and other major industrial corporations — lies ahead. To meet that challenge successfully will require a new and different federal role: a new industrial policy.

Conclusion

It should be clear that I strongly believe that the United States does badly need an industrial policy. Indeed, I am convinced that as a long-term goal, we need an entirely new "economic agenda." The key elements of that agenda should be: a commitment to full employment, including a guaranteed right to a decent job to every individual who is willing and able to work; comprehensive economic planning in support of this objective and the full and productive utilization of our nation's resources; a rational energy policy, which emphasizes development of safe, non-polluting renewable alternative energy supplies as well as conservation; national health insurance, which provides adquate medical care to every American, as a matter of right; an active labor market policy, including among other things plant closing legislation which provides for mandatory advance notice, show-cause hearings, transfer rights, adequate income maintenance and fringe benefit protection, retraining and relocation assistance, conversion to alternative production and community redevelopment assistance; and finally, and perhaps most difficult of all to achieve, thorough-going democratization of corporate decision-making. Though the current political climate will not make achievement of any of these goals easy, the underlying problems which give rise to the need for this new economic blueprint are bound to persist.

It is as an adjunct to these and other needed reforms to get our economy and society moving again that "Industrial Policy" could play a meaningful role. This will require among other things, that the government develop the capacity to anticipate and to plan. It is necessary, for example, to know well in advance which industries will be in crisis. It is necessary to know specific plants and specific communities most likely to be in trouble. It is necessary to develop and implement coherent plans ahead of time, to counter the effects of these dislocations before they occur.

The experience of other industrialized nations indicates that while none of this is easy, it *can* be done. In the U.S., we have failed even to make a good-faith try, as workers and communities are sacrificed to mystical and outdated notions of "free enterprise."

The corporate agenda is simply not in the best interests of the vast majority of Americans. It is neither necessary or fair to ask the American public to give up hard-won protections of their health and safety, the purity of their food and drugs, or the quality of their environment, on the altar of "reindustrialization." It is neither necessary or fair to further cut corporate income taxes via increased investment tax credits, eased depreciation rules, or other untargeted means, while the tax burden on ordinary citizens continues to mount. It is neither necessary nor fair for those millions of working Americans who are struggling to make ends meet to submit to inequitable wage restraints while profits are permitted to "roam free." It is neither necessary nor fair for American workers to be threatened, coerced and denied their right to organize, so that corporations can trim labor costs in a "union-free environment." Nor should our millions of elderly, disabled, unemployed and impoverished be forced to endure cutbacks in vital social programs under the guise of "belt-tightening" to promote "reindustrialization" while military expenditures continue to increase.

None of these things is necessary or fair; nor are they inevitable. There *is* an alternative.

Failing Industries: The Role of Government

By Fletcher L. Byrom, Chairman of the Board,
Koppers Company, Inc.

Let me cast my arguments in question-and-answer form.

Many of the questions that appear below have been culled from the hundreds I have faced as the head of a large industrial corporation and as a so-called "business spokesman." Their merit lies in the fact that they represent the real (as opposed to theoretical) concerns of a fairly large and diverse collection of people. The other questions I have supplied myself in order to permit me to say, without being too stuffy about it, certain things I believe ought to be said.

Many of the answers that appear below are based on statements I have gone on record with, in print, on platforms or in person-to-person exchange. Their merit lies in the fact that they have been tempered in the heat of debate. The other answers I have cooked up fresh for this present offering.

I begin with the basic question, implied in the title assigned:

What is the role of government in failing industries?

The question can be taken in two ways, and I choose to preserve the ambiguity, which I find useful.

First, what is government's role once industrial failure becomes imminent or actual? For the most part, I believe, government's role should be restricted to dealing with the *consequences* of failure as they affect society. At a time when our options are necessarily limited by economic considerations and its own structural flaws, government should not conduct interventions that frustrate the successful working of market forces.

Second, and more worth pursuing, is the question of how government contributes to the failure of industry. Does government, in fact, help to generate industrial failure? The evidence is various, and strong, that it does. We have only to look at such areas as tax policy, regulation, antitrust activity, and the general environment in which industries must operate under a spreading bureaucracy.

Can we tackle those one at a time? Let's start with tax policy.

I take my beginning text from a statement issued last January by the Committee for Economic Development, which took part of *its* text from something published in 1978 by Robert S. Kaplan, dean of Carnegie-Mellon's Graduate School of Industrial Administration. Here's how one passage goes:

> The governments of Japan, West Germany, and France . . . have provided special accelerated depreciation allowances to approved investments in new technology (Japan) or to plant and equipment devoted to research and development (Germany) or used for scientific and technical research (France). In Japan, companies that form joint research associations in certain industries can immediately expense the cost of contributions for new machinery and equipment or a new facility. In Germany, a 7.5 percent tax-free cash subsidy is provided for investment in R&D facilities; and in France, special companies formed to perform research and development or apply innovative processes receive highly favored tax treatment on all kinds of activity.

Japan sweetens the pot further with a 20 percent tax credit for certain R&D expenditures. In Germany, if you as an industrialist get supplementary income from scientific activities, you may be taxed at half the normal rate. The French apply the long-term capital gains rate to sales of patent rights and technical and manufacturing processes. That rate is only 15 percent.

This represents a difference in tax philosophy that puts American companies at a serious disadvantage in competition with our major trading partners. I will not believe we are serious about revitalizing our industries until we come up with a tax policy that gives individuals and businesses the incentive to take the kind of long-term risk that is inherent in most investment for technological advance.

All that relates to R&D investments. What about capital investment generally?

We have in our system something known as depreciation accounting. This is supposed to provide us with the funds we need to cover the costs of wearing out our plants and equipment. It is not a gift from the national treasury; it is what we are allowed to keep out of current sales revenue for the purpose. It works fine when prices are stable — which is to say seldom. In an inflationary economy, such as we have been going through, it makes no sense at all. If all companies were taking full depreciation on capital investment, a great many of them would not have the resources to pay dividends. When they do pay dividends, they are presiding over their own liquidation.

One study indicates that underdepreciation and phantom inventory profits cost corporations $150 billion or more in excess taxes over the past six years, all of it due to inflation.

What would you consider a more equitable approach, since no one really knows what the rate of inflation will be from one year to the next?

The question almost answers itself. The CED calls more rapid capital recovery allowance "the number-one priority measure to stimulate investment in new plant and equipment." Myself, I'd like to see industry permitted to write off its capital investments almost immediately, say in a year or two, provided the depreciation taken does not exceed the investment in new plant and equipment during the period in question.

It would be a tremendous stimulus for the kind of investment we need to turn our economy around, boost our productivity and strengthen our competitive position in international trade.

What you've been talking about seems to apply mainly to large manufacturing industries.

Every businessman and every individual has his own horror story to tell when it comes to tax policy. Right now, it's the turn of the publishing industry. A recent Supreme Court decision had the effect of ruling that it can no longer record sharp writedowns on the values of its inventories for tax purposes. It has to pay taxes without charging off slow-moving inventories unless it gets rid of them one way or another. The government doesn't care how you do it — sell them at a loss, give them away if anyone will have them, dump them at sea.

Now, anyone who is familiar with the book business knows it is customary for publishers to keep large stocks on hand. For one thing, there are certain titles that keep on selling year after year; J.D. Salinger hasn't published anything new since the 1960s, but people keep buying his books by the hundreds of thousands annually. For another thing, nobody can predict how many copies a book will sell, so it has always been considered cheaper to overprint and store copies than to have to go back on press.

What this new ruling means is that, unless we get some corrective legislation soon, researchers won't have access to backlists of scholarly works. Publishers will steer clear of manuscripts they might formerly have bought in order to meet the needs of small but important audiences. A lot of authors will never get into print.

I don't know whether you'd classify an unpublished author as a failing industry, but that's certainly a poignant reminder of how tax policy often works against the public good.

And how do you get rid of millions of books? My inclination would be to put a match to them, weeping all the while, but that would get me into trouble with the environmental people.

Which leads us neatly to the next topic — regulation.

The statistician's dream. You can hardly pick up a newspaper these days without finding something about how much regulations cost us, in money, time and lost opportunity. What I read the other day was that the number of lawyers in this country tripled in the 1970s, to almost 500,000. I'd be willing to bet that a large part of that army sprang into being because someone sowed the dragon's teeth of regulation.

A book published this year* tells us how pervasive the phenomenon has become. It cites estimates that business has to spend $32 billion a year to comply with the government's paperwork demands and then says that figure may be understated by a factor of four. It says government spends more than $43 billion a year to print, process, compile and store federal forms. "In all," it says, "an estimated $100 billion a year — and many believe the figure is higher — is sucked from our economy to comply with this paperwork passion."

The decade of the 1970s set all kinds of records, with the passage of more than 120 major regulatory laws and the establishment of 21 major agencies, more than twice as many as in any previous decade. The agencies were not only more numerous, but bigger. The Food and Drug Administration almost doubled its staff. At the Equal Employment Opportunity Commission, the jump was from 780 employees in 1970 to almost 4,000 today.

Hasn't there been a countering movement, to cut back on the number, size and powers of the agencies?

There has, and it has been supported strongly by political elements who otherwise have little in common. But regulatory agencies tend to develop their own constituencies. They tend to grow and to reach out for more and more areas in which to operate. They tend to gather to their side supporters who magnify their importance and shield them against attack.

Why is this tolerated?

Gabriel Hauge, who delivered the first Fairless Memorial Lec-

Fat City: How Washington Wastes Your Taxes, by Donald Lambro; Regnery-Gateway, Inc., 1980.

ture in 1963 and who himself served time in government, may have put his finger on it when he said, "In dealing with the electorate, minorities punish but majorities seldom protect."

This is a fairly new development in the history of our political process. It has resulted in a behind-the-scenes government that enjoys maximum power with minimum accountability. It has brought us organizations that preserve themselves in existence long after the problems they were created to handle have disappeared. Edmund S. Muskie, before he gave up his seat in the Senate to become Secretary of State, asked, "Why can't liberals start raising hell about a government so big, so complex, so expensive, and so unresponsive that it's dragging down every good program we've worked for?"

Maybe the reason people don't really revolt is that they view regulation as only a nuisance, while the things regulated — things like industrial safety, air quality, ambient noise — are menaces.

People respond to what affects them immediately and directly. In 1955, when T. Coleman Andrews was commissioner of the Internal Revenue Service, he was asked to comment on the fact that 12 million people had come to his agency for help with their tax forms the year before. He said, "There is something wrong with any law that causes that many people to have to take a whole day off from their jobs to find out how to comply." He understood what hit home with the public.

I wish it were true that regulation is only a nuisance, but the truth is that regulation, whose advocates profess to serve the public interest, often harms the public interest and certainly does not proceed from consultation with the public. We had an experience of our own at Koppers to illustrate this fact. At one point, the Federal Trade Commission made us stop what it called "a predatory pricing practice" for a certain chemical. Current profit levels for that chemical were acceptable. Our sin was that we were unwilling to raise its price to a higher level in order to keep an inefficient producer alive, thereby permitting him to a share of the market that could be served more efficiently by us. Naturally, it was the consumer who eventually lost — the very consumer whose interests are supposed to be protected by these regulatory agencies.

People are beginning to learn that it is they who must eventually pay for such things as seat belts and catalytic converters, but the cost of most regulation is hidden from the public. Let me give you two examples.

A few years ago, Edgar Speer, of U.S. Steel, gave us some figures for his industry. He said that every dollar spent for pollution control equipment added 12 to 15 cents to annual operating costs. I have seen one report that puts the 1979 figure at 18 cents. This charge adds nothing to productivity. The question is whether the social benefit achieved is of a magnitude that warrants the additional cost.

The effects of regulation in medicine have sometimes been devastating. It now takes at least seven years and as much as $60 million to bring a new drug onto the market. The result is that Americans have to wait for years after life-saving drugs are available in other countries and that the costs for such drugs keep rising. Some drugs never reach the market because there are too few potential "customers" to justify the expense of development, so that one is wise to contract a popular disease and avoid the exotic.

I hope nobody thinks that these examples represent only nuisances or that the costs stop at the steel companies and the pharmaceutical manufacturers. Eventually, it is the consumer who pays.

But you're talking, to a large extent, about areas in which the purpose of regulation is to protect the citizenry from risk. Isn't that a proper function of government?

It is. All I'm saying is that we haven't set up a system to internalize the costs of regulation. Until we do that — until we let industry pass on these costs and let people see in advance what they are paying for regulation — we will not have satisfied the conditions of our democratic process. After all, when people can choose whether or not they want to spend their dollars for such and such an intervention, this is a form of voting, which is consonant with democracy. When the decisions are made by bureaucrats, that looks to me like authoritarianism.

Beyond that, the regulators seem to be working more and more toward an insistence upon zero-risk environments. I have a feeling that if fire had been invented in our time, it would have been squelched by EPA on grounds of smoke emission and by OSHA on grounds of burned fingers.

Herbert A. Simon, the Carnegie-Mellon professor who won the 1978 Nobel Prize in economics, once commented on the struggle over automotive emissions. "The standards looked reasonable to us," he said, "but maybe we're paying too much for the last gram of control." He said the emphasis on cleaning up the internal combustion engine has undoubtedly reduced the research that might have gone to other power plants, and he concluded, "Not to look at other options, in effect, was a decision that shifted billions."

How do we determine what costs people will be willing to bear in order to enjoy the kind of environment the ecologists tell us we should strive for?

Where appropriate, response-to-market will do it for us. Otherwise, short of a national referendum on every decision, it's not easy. Judgment and common sense have to guide us. One man who possesses a fair share of both is the futurist Herman Kahn. Here is what he said in a discussion last year:

Yes, people are clearly willing to spend money on environmental protection. But are they willing to spend a lot of money to preserve the snail darter? Absolutely not. Are they willing to spend a lot of money to preserve the Houston toad? Hell, no. Whooping cranes? Sure. Golden eagles? Sure. Whales? Sure.

Mr. Kahn says he has a theory: "To win public support, it has got to be a very big, very ugly, have big wings, or be cuddly."

That's not unrelated to what we've been talking about. It seems to be part of the regulator's credo that we can achieve a world absolutely without hazard, especially if somebody else has to pay for it. The extra cost of eliminating all risk, rather than defining an acceptable level of risk, is often enormous. And the resources we use to do that in one area are resources we won't have available to usefully act in other areas.

Regardless of whether we finally realize the impossibility of zero-risk programs, there will always be a certain amount of demand for regulation. What alternative do you see for the present system?

Many corrective measures are needed, from mandatory cost-benefit analyses that will permit us to allocate our resources wisely to "sunset laws" that will overcome the sheer inertia by which many regulatory programs remain in force long after they have outlived their original purpose.

My chief complaint is that the regulators tell us not what our destination should be, but what roads we should travel. Nearly every one of the regulatory programs that have emerged in the past decade is designed to bypass the market system through the imposition of formulas and schedules prefabricated on the bureaucratic assembly lines. When I hire someone to wash my car, I don't specify what kind of soap he shall use or how hot the water shall be. All I ask is that he gets my car clean at a reasonable price within a reasonable period of time without injury to the finish.

But government doesn't operate that way. For instance, it should work to control pollution by making industry pay for unacceptable departures from established standards. That incentive would inspire industry to devise the most efficient ways to meet those standards. It would undoubtedly stimulate the development of better tools and procedures than those now dictated by government.

Murray L. Weidenbaum, director of the Center for the Study of American Business at Washington University, has offered some thoughts on this issue. Speaking on regulations for job safety, he says:

> Excessively detailed regulations are often merely a substitute for hard policy decisions. Rather than stressing the issuance of citations to employers who fail to fill out forms correctly or who do not post the required notices, emphasis should be placed on the regulation of those employers with high and rising accident rates.

Fines might be levied, he says, whereupon some companies might find it more efficient to change work rules, others to buy new equipment and still others to retrain workers. Each would have sought the solution most properly fitted to its circumstances and needs, instead of being forced into a common mold of compliance.

You spoke of letting industry pass on the cost of regulation. Doesn't that happen automatically?

It doesn't happen when government "jawbones" industry out of compensatory price increases and it doesn't happen when we have to compete with foreign industries that are not subject to the same kind of regulation.

Proportionately, it is the smaller companies that are hit hardest by regulation. They cannot afford the batteries of lawyers, accountants and other specialists who typically inhabit the large corporations. James McKevitt, chief counsel for the National Federation of Independent Businesses, says his 445,000 members "have to spend 15 to 20 percent of their time every week simply filling out various forms requested by an endless variety of Federal agencies." The mortality rate is higher at that level, and that's what I mean by irony — that one arm of government condemns the process whereby smaller companies are merged into larger companies while another arm hastens that process by making it harder for small companies to stay in business. I wonder how many potential IBM's we have lost because their founders were too discouraged and too distracted by the necessity to toe the regulatory line.

This seems a good point at which to turn to your third area of dissatisfaction — antitrust activity.

IBM is a good place to start this discussion. At a time when we in America have lost our technological leadership in a number of industries we used to dominate — steel, rubber, consumer electronics and the like — we still manifest unmistakable superiority in the world of computers. Am I the only one who finds it absolutely ridiculous that our government has pushed the greatest antitrust effort in its history to break up the company that has put us at the top of that particular heap?

Isn't the original premise of antitrust still valid, to prevent the formation of monopolies and combinations that can dictate prices, offer inferior merchandise and limit the number of selections because they have no effective competition?

The premise might have been valid when the Sherman Antitrust Act was passed in 1890, when American industry operated largely within a domestic market. We don't live in that kind of world today. You don't have to hold a club over General Motors; the Japanese do it for us. No American automaker can dictate to the market, not even if it should be the only one in the country, for that would immediately create a consumer resistance that foreign companies would be quick to spot and cater to. The discipline of the international market place makes more sense than domestic antitrust and is practically instantaneous when compared with the slow deliberations of our courts.

But we do still hold a club over General Motors, and that has made for all sorts of difficulty. GM has for years enjoyed a significantly higher return on investment than Ford or Chrysler. In the normal course of things, it might have lowered its prices, or given its workers greater benefits, or done any number of other things that would serve the public interest. To have done so, however, would have invited government action far worse than the kind Koppers faced when it tried to hold down the price of that chemical I was talking about. And the result has been that all of our automakers have gone through difficult times, with one of them close to the brink, because their own government inhibited the industry from the kind of growth and combination you need to compete in today's world.

But we're talking about an industry that engages the entire nation, economically, politically, socially and even emotionally. It accounts for one out of every six or seven jobs. A vast complex of related industries depends on its welfare. And Americans love their cars. Our society is built on the assumed right of independent and individual transportation. It's understandable that government would want to keep a tight grip on things. Doesn't that make the auto industry a special case when it comes to antitrust?

Not at all — only one of the most conspicuous. Take steel. It is preposterous for government to insist that we spread our steel industry among 30 producers when three or four might give us all we need in the way of competitive pressure at home and would permit us to operate under the new ground rules of the international market place. If the steel industry were rationalized, we would be producing 60 percent of the nation's steel at 10 plants served by deepwater ports.

A recent international listing shows Russia owning the largest blast furnace in the world, with the cautionary that they may have other giant installations not yet announced. It is not until you get to the ninth and tenth positions in that listing that you find the American entries. Ahead of us are three in Japan, two in the United Kingdom, and one each in France and Italy. Behind us — close behind — are blast furnaces in West Germany, Japan again, and China.

What this means is that our government has thwarted the combinations needed to develop true economies of scale. It does so not only by forbidding mergers, but by preventing cooperative action between companies. At a time of worldwide coke shortages, for instance, the steel companies should be joining forces to build large coke batteries that could serve several of them at once. By law, they cannot. The automobile companies should be joining forces to conduct research in fuel efficiency and emission controls. By law, they cannot. Lester C. Thurow, professor of economics and management at Massachusetts Institute of Technology, has called for abolition of the antitrust laws, saying we "cannot afford to force American companies to independently invent the same wheel when they should be engaging in co-operative research and development projects."

You've talked about tax policy, regulation and antitrust activity. Does that leave anything for your fourth bugaboo, "the general environment in which industries must operate under a spreading bureaucracy?"

All those factors are intertwined, and it is not easy to sort out cause and effect. If I had to name the most important single effect — the one factor in our economic environment that will most influence our future as a society — it would be inflation.

Theodore H. White addresses himself to this subject in his autobiographical *In Search of History*. He tells of how the Chinese were the first to issue paper notes that passed as money, setting them "off on a course no one could control." He traces the various dynasties, down to Kublai Khan's Cathay, which "died in a blizzard of useless paper money." "Since then," he writes, "almost always, whenever a government has perished it has done so in a paroxysm of inflation. From the Sung dynasty to the French Revolution, from the Confederacy of the United States to the Weimar Republic, inflation has accompanied the death rattle."

Inflation, that great Thief of All Pockets, works in mysterious ways its mischief to perform. Martin Feldstein, president of the National Bureau of Economic Research, says that between 1954 and 1965, the effective tax take on real income paid by corporations, shareholders and creditors was cut by 12 points, from 66 percent to 54 percent, through rate reductions, accelerated depreciation and the investment tax credit. Accelerated inflation, however, has brought the tax burden back to 66 percent, as against the 43 percent that would obtain today if prices had remained stable. This means, Professor Feldstein says, that "what Congress and the Treasury have done, inflation has undone."

Wage earners also suffer. According to the National Taxpayers Union, a 10 percent raise these days means a 16 percent rise in taxes even though Congress has not boosted rates since the early 1950s. The organization says that 70 percent of American families have less buying power than they had in 1969 as a result of higher prices and the "ratchet effect" that sends them into higher tax brackets.

What solution do you see?

There is no single solution, but we will never solve inflation until we reverse the government's bias toward consumption and do something about productivity. According to the CED, the growth of our manufacturing productivity over the past two decades has ranged between one-third and one-half of the rate for Japan, Germany and France. In 1979, productivity in our private business sector, which has shown an absolute decline only twice since the end of World War II, fell by almost 1 percent.

We are not going to turn this situation around simply by asking people to work harder. What we need is more in the way of equipment, plant and tools. And that will take money. We now put only 17 percent of our gross national product into investment, less than any of our trading partners except for the United Kingdom. And even that, according to Martin Feldstein, boils down to "only a measly 3 percent" devoted to greater productivity when you take out the amounts needed to replace exsting facilities, buy housing and accumulate inventories.

What kind of money are we talking about to get American productivity back to where it should be?

Estimates vary. Willard C. Butcher, president of Chase Manhattan Bank, last year said the need for capital formation would amount to $4 trillion in the 1980s. That's trillions. I speak as one who grew up in a period when "billion" was a strange and incomprehensible figure. A study published by the New York Stock Exchange at the end of 1979 said we would need $1.8 trillion in 1972 dollars for the economy to perform at even minimally acceptable levels in the decade ahead. *U.S. News and World Report* says the transportation industry alone will require a 10-year total of $2 trillion.

Where that money will come from — I wish I knew. What I do know is that the core challenge confronting us today is the rapid depletion of our capital base. We consume our wealth as fast as we create it, like a farmer who fails to set aside seed for future crops. What we need, if I may mix metaphors, is the fiscal equivalent of the Scarsdale diet.

A few years ago, you spoke of "the strange alchemy whereby government transmutes the solid gold of promise into the common lead of failure." Do you have any clues as to why this happens?

I thought you'd never ask. You see, my daily routine doesn't leave much time for whimsy. Especially, I have never been able to indulge in the conspiracy theories that fascinate so many of our citizens. I accepted the Warren Commission's findings from the day they were published and I never did believe Senator McCarthy had those lists of card-carrying subversives he talked about.

Still, I like to imagine what would happen if I had been sent to these shores a long time ago from a galaxy far, far away.

Let's say that my assignment is to weaken the American society so that it will be ready for takeover. Very quickly, I realize that my best means to this end is to destroy the economy. This must be done quietly, so subtly that no one fully realizes what is going on until it is too late to do anything about it.

Once my androids are securely positioned in the proper bureaus and agencies, I seek out the primary target. I perceive that one of the distinguishing features of the society we have infiltrated is the business corporation. I see that it is an institutional form that has evolved naturally in response to need, a mechanism that the Terrestrials have worked out in order to get certain things done — to make products, to provide services, to channel labor into useful structures, to create wealth out of raw resources. It must, therefore, be eliminated.

Once my mission is well under way, I report back to the Emperor. The corporations are already showing signs of debility, I say. The Force is no longer with them. Whenever two or more of them seek to join together in order to enjoy the economies that come with greater size, they are battered down in the courts. Gnawing away at their vitals is a spreading infestation of taxes, the more severe symptoms of which are masked by inflation. Further sapping their strength is a barrage of regulations that add to cost without helping productivity, often harming the consumers they purport to help.

Victory is within sight, my report concludes, the light at the end of the tunnel. What I do not tell the Emperor is that little of this was attributable to me. For the most part, they did it to themselves!

You don't get off that easy. What do you think really accounts for what you once called government's "Midas touch in reverse"?

John Fischer, the late editor of *Harper's* magazine, may have had the answer. Speaking of our federal government, he wrote:
> The basic design, patented 200 years ago, was splendid for . . . the governing of a small, isolated, simple, rural society. Over the years, [we] have tinkered with it, adding gadgets, bureaus, commissions, and power steering until the old chassis was completely overloaded. As a consequence, it is close to breakdown. . . . It is inadequate for a society grown huge and hideously complex.

For myself, I look upon our federal government as a managerial nightmare. It is like a 200-year-old house that has had a succession of new heating plants, new wiring, new plumbing — without ever ripping out the old heating plants, the old wiring, the old plumbing. The basic design is good, but the structure is being destroyed by "improvements."

Aside from government's structural imperfections, we must remember that we are dealing not simply with an inanimate complex, but with very real human beings who display some very real human inclinations. This is particularly evident in the field of regulation.

One of these inclinations is a tendency to play it safe by demanding 100 percent performance when 98 or 95 percent might be perfectly acceptable and would get the job done more quickly and efficiently. I can wash three windows satisfactorily in the time that it takes a perfectionist to wash one.

Further, there is what we might call the "negative invisible." I spoke of the long and costly delays pharmaceutical companies face when they seek approval for new drugs. A good part of that delay must be traceable to a mentality that says you're more likely to be attacked for approving a drug that proves harmful than you are for withholding approval from a drug that might save lives. In other words, what people don't know can't hurt you.

Finally, there is the impulse to justify one's job, to do something, anything. When Nikita Krushchev was premier of the U.S.S.R., he said: "Politicians are the same all over. They promise to build a bridge even where there is no river." Imagine that you are a bureaucrat assigned to oversee the regulation of a certain industry. And imagine that industry's performance is beyond reproach. What are you going to do when you get to the office every day? Will you fill out a report saying you found nothing to criticize? How boring! And where are you going to look for your next job?

Paul H. Weaver, an editor of *Fortune* magazine, speaks of the arguments developed by certain scholars to the effect that "the real bias of the regulatory agencies is not that they favor the regulated but that they have an enormous stake in regulating per se, and that the 'special interests' the agencies really serve are those involved in the regulatory process itself — lawyers, judges, environmental consultants, business lobbyists, and so forth." The real purpose of government regulation, he says, "is not to correct the deficiencies of markets but to transcend markets altogether," so that government regulation becomes not economic policy, but social policy. And he refers to a "prodigality with other people's resources" that prevails in the regulatory process.

Aren't there bureaucrats who fall outside these patterns?

Of course there are, many, many of them. But the pressures must be hard to resist. Jean-Francois Revel, the French educator and biologist, once wrote:

> The contemporary free state is called upon . . . at once to intervene and to keep hands off. That is why wielding power subject to that conflict is so trying on those in public office. The strain is bound to shatter the mind of anyone who is not unconquerably stolid or already demented.

Hasn't government intervention been in some measure a response to popular frustrations? People see flaws in the world they occupy and they can't believe that a society this great can't set things right. More and more, you hear, "If we can put men on the moon, why can't we" — *and then name your favorite cause.*

One of America's most popular television series is M*A*S*H, and a recurrent situation in that series shows the helicopters bringing in fresh batches of wounded soldiers, whereupon the commanding officer summons his medical staff with the call, "Triage!" What "triage" means is that they must allocate their resources as wisely as possible. The most serious treatable injuries will get the promptest attention. Others will await their turn. And a few will be abandoned, because their cases are hopeless and any effort applied to them would dilute the effectiveness of treatment for the others.

45

Any consideration of industrial failure must take into account this notion of triage. Our resources are not unlimited.

As it happens, that fact has been called harshly to our attention recently under circumstances that involve both medicine and economics. The government has announced that, with few exceptions, Medicare will no longer cover the cost of heart transplant operations, which run an average of $100,000 each. Health and Human Services Secretary Patricia Roberts Harris says:

I don't like the idea of assessing the value of a human life. I don't think that can be done. At the same time, we have to find out what the costs are. We have to ask, "Will we buy this or will we buy something else?"

Right now, some people are questioning the department's artificial kidney treatment program, which covers almost 60,000 people and whose cost keeps escalating, now running over $1 billion a year.

Is this affordable? Who can say? And what if another expensive procedure comes along? What if we discover that a certain disease can be controlled only by sending the patient off for a three-month stay in the low-gravity, vacuum environment of the moon's surface?

These are not merely academic questions. Louise R. Russell, a member of the staff of Brookings Institution's Economic Studies program, has written about the debate over national health insurance and cost control. She says:

If we decide to limit the flow of dollars into medical care, then we must decide what the limits will be and choose methods for deciding what to do, and for whom, within these limits. . . . If, on the other hand, we reject rationing for now and decide to continue to provide everything that is needed, we must expect further large increases in costs, keeping in mind that a dollar spent on medical care is a dollar that cannot be spent on something else. The choice is as much a choice between problems as between solutions.

Have we wandered from the subject of failing industries?

We have not. Similar principles apply. We have to ask ourselves how much we can do, how far we should go to prop up ailing industries at the expense of healthy industries. If there is one lesson we Americans should have learned during these troubled years, it is this: it may be true that we can have *anything* we want, but we cannot have *everything* we want. We must choose.

Developing countries have been accused, with some justification, of demanding high standards of living, usually under socialist forms of government, without being willing to go through the hard periods of capital formation and plowback that characterized economic history in the West. Isn't it possible that we have been guilty of a comparable sin in America, in such areas as medical care, unemployment benefits, retirement programs and the search for absolute freedom from risk in the environment and in the work place? Our leaders do us no favor when they imply that we can have all these things to the full at little or no cost.

Do you ever entertain the thought that part of the criticism of government may come from businessmen — present company excepted, of course — seeking excuses for the results of their own mismanagement?

Statistically, that's a possibility. But it's not uncommon, either, for the business community to criticize its own shortcomings. As far back as 1921, H.L. Mencken called the businessman "the only man above the hangman and the scavenger who is forever apologizing for his occupation."

Actually, I think American business has much to be proud of. Within our lifetime, it rallied virtually overnight to arm the forces of the free world in their victorious war against what seemed like the overwhelming strength of the Axis powers. It gave us a standard of living unparalleled in history. In the 1970s, it boosted the total number of jobs in this country by 24 percent, a figure unsurpassed by any other major industrial economy.

I think future historians may compare our performance in these times to that of the Norse god Thor on his voyage to Jotunheim, land of the giants. Thor threw his mighty hammer, whose blow had always been fatal before, at the head of the sleeping giant Utgard-Loki, who only yawned in response. He was humiliated in a wrestling match with an ancient crone. He was unable to drain a drinking horn of ordinary proportions. Only later did he learn that his hammer had struck and cracked a mountain the giant was using for a pillow, that the ancient crone was Old Age, which downs all men, that the drinking horn was connected to a river that he almost emptied before he was through.

For Thor, read our modern businessman. For those tricky giants, read our modern bureaucrats.

Surely there are factors in industrial failure other than government intervention.

47

Granted. A corporation may fail because it doesn't properly manage its capital structure. It depends too much upon debt, and can't service its debt in bad times. It is unable to raise equity.

A corporation may fail because its enthusiasm for making a product is not matched by the public's enthusiasm for buying that product.

A corporation may fail because it expands in a business that has matured and that is being displaced by new products. Kerosene lanterns and iceboxes come to mind.

Those are classic perils. They have always existed. Now we have a new development that induces failure: intervention by society, through government, into the operations of the corporation.

It is one thing, and a good thing, to say that we must have no price collusion, no fraudulent advertising, no harmful products, no dumping of dangerous wastes.

But society can also impose price controls. Working through government, it can prevent combinations intended to provide economies of scale where technology calls for greater capacity than any one corporation can provide. Society can tell you that the discharge of a given pollutant must be reduced to zero — that you must protect workers by eliminating discharges instead of providing them with protective equipment — that you must pay a minimum wage, regardless of what that does to unskilled people who are essentially unemployable at that level — that you must price materials, such as gasoline, below their true value, so that the consumption of these materials distorts natural market forces in ways that will eventually lead to a costly reckoning.

Roy L. Ash, who first came to notice as co-founder of Litton Industries and then as director of the Office of Management and Budget, a man who has studied the worlds of business and government, tells us what has happened:

> Where the earlier regulatory agencies were predicated on the proposition that a market economy was our desired mechanism of production, distribution, and exchange and then were charged with making up for various problems and deficiencies in that mechanism — such as the need to deal with "natural" monopolies and to provide adequate information — the newer agencies are based on the premise that a market economy is not necessarily a desirable means. To a large extent, the newer agencies exist to direct business conduct toward socially "good" goals, with little regard for

the disruption of the market economy, and thus cost.

The most conspicuous recent example of government intervention seems not to have harmed a major industry, but to have rescued it. Do you approve of the measures so far taken in the Chrysler bailout?

I don't want to get hung up on the Chrysler case, or even on the automobile industry generally. Others are in trouble. Steel is a perfect example of an industry that will have failing corporations because of government actions and policies, through interventions in the collective bargaining process, pollution control, health and safety rules, wage and price pressures, and always the threat of antitrust action. Back in 1977, I delivered myself of these words:

> We will come eventually to the point where this country must decide whether it really needs a steel industry. . . . I give us 10 years. By the end of that time, I believe, we will be past the point of no return in terms of the ability of the private sector to fund the modernization and replacement of plant.

I predicted a similar fate for other industries — the utilities, some nonferrous metals. That was three years ago, and I see no reason to alter my timetable. Just recently, in fact, Senators Schweiker and Heinz unveiled a document written by the official scheduled to supervise the reinstated trigger-price program to protect our steel producers from unfair foreign competition. That document, according to newspaper reports, describes steel as a "lemon industry" and urges the Administration to "ease the transition of labor and capital into more profitable enterprises."

To respond more directly to your question, I will say no, I did not approve of the Chrysler bailout. I recognize that the automotive industry has become, in Murray Weidenbaum's phrase, "the most heavily regulated industry in America," so that government's action is like throwing a lifeline to the passenger it has just pushed overboard. But I do not believe that we serve ourselves well by propping up our weakest producers. There may be some success stories, but experience here and abroad tells us that this approach, as a policy for adjusting to long-term change, is most unlikely to achieve benefits that will exceed the costs to the communities immediately involved or to society generally.

What do we do about those communities?

The real problem with arguments for saving specific plants in local areas is that benefits are expressed strictly in terms of the number of jobs saved. Hardly anyone ever talks about the jobs that are *not* created in unassisted areas because the resources which would have been available for that purpose have been diverted to salvage operations. There is almost no discussion of the tax-provided expenditures for such salvage operations and the consequently reduced availability of resources for plant and equipment needed to raise the nation's productivity and to stimulate economic growth.

Do you object to government aid for industries whose failure is due to unfair competition from abroad?

I do not object to such aid as a holding action while the question of unfairness is being argued, but I would want to be very clear about the nature of that aid and I would want to be sure about any definition of "unfair." We hear more and more talk these days about "protectionism," a return to the old days of high tariffs, stiff import quotas and other barriers to free trade. Sheila Page, of London's National Institute for Economic and Social Research, says the portion of world trade subject to tariffs, quotas or other barriers has risen from 40 percent in 1974 to 46 percent in 1980. And Peter Coldrick, secretary of the European Trade Union Confederation, sees the trend accelerating as unemployment rises. "These pressures are inevitable when people are losing their jobs," he says.

The prospect frightens me. The Smoot-Hawley Tariff Act of 1930, signed by President Hoover against the protest of more than a thousand reputable economists, helped to bring on a global depression and gave us World War II for dessert. What another return to protectionism in any form might bring may be too horrible to contemplate.

Isn't it conceivable that government acts because it sees the failure of a major corporation as its own failure, or at least fears the public will perceive it as such?

It's tragic when any element of our society regards the loss of a single corporation as a symptom of the entire system's defeat. Failure in business is like death in nature, a way of cleaning out. I can't imagine a healthy economy in which no one ever went out of business, any more than I can imagine a healthy biosphere in which nothing ever died. Death is nature's way of making room for new and better forms. Immortality would mean the end of the line for progress.

We worry about big companies going out of business, but there are thousands of small companies going bankrupt every year and we hardly notice their passing. Last year, we had more than 7,500 business failures in this country. Most of them went quietly to their graves, like Thomas Gray's flower, "born to blush unseen, and waste its sweetness on the desert air."

On the specific issue of the automobile industry, we tend to forget that that industry once had dozens of companies that are no longer around. Within my own lifetime, I have seen the passing of the Peerless and the Pierce-Arrow, the Essex and the Hudson Super Six, the Studebaker and the Packard, the Crosley and the Henry J. Most of these succumbed to a simple rule of technology, which requires that you must make more and more of less and less in order to survive. Even among those still with us today, there has been many an in-family burial; General Motors had the La Salle and the Corvair, Ford had the Edsel of eternal fame, and Chrysler, long before the present crisis, had the Airflow and the De Soto.

Hasn't the automobile industry brought a lot of its troubles on its own head? The other day, I ran across a New York Times parody of Tennyson's "Locksley Hall," updated to 1971, long before the current troubles. It was titled "Detroit Doggerel", and it went:

"For I looked into the future
"Far as human eye could see,
"Saw a vision of the world
"And all the wonder that would be.

"Saw the freeway filled with traffic,
"No mass transit, only cars,
"200 million Fords and Chevys,
"The urban planners drunk in bars."

I wonder whether any other industry has ever been the victim of so many misconceptions. As Josh Billings said, "It is better to know nothing than to know what ain't so."

It is not true that the industry never understood what the public wanted. What the public wanted not too many years ago was something that would transport a couple with two children, a dog and a boat to the seashore for two weeks. And what really brought the industry to crisis was the government policy that told people they could always count on a plentiful supply of cheap gasoline. This led to two- and three-car families and the notion that one could set one's home down 40 miles away from one's place of work and make the trip both ways five days a week without access to public transportation.

Much of the story is told in a superb article by William Tucker, a contributing editor of *Harper's*, in the November 1980 issue of that magazine. The key, he says, was the 1975 Energy Policy and Conservation Act — an ironic name — by which "Congress actually *lowered* the price of gasoline and promised that Americans would not have to pay more than an additional ten cents per gallon for the rest of the decade and perhaps even beyond that," in spite of inescapable evidence that "*nothing except* gasoline prices has had even the slightest effect in making Americans decide whether to buy small or large cars." He quotes Secretary of Transportation Neil Goldschmidt, who says, "Because the political courage to deregulate the price of oil was not present in 1975, the U.S. government allowed the nation to go from importing one-third of its oil to nearly half, and the opportunity to make a gradual shift of the nation's automobile fleet from larger to smaller cars was lost."

Mr. Tucker goes on to demolish the series of myths about the industry. Detroit was not late on the scene with compact cars; the Corvair, Falcon and Valiant appeared in 1959 and were immediate successes, helping to drive the import share of market down to 4 percent by 1962. Detroit's product was not inferior in quality; in 1970, foreign cars, although only 15 percent of the American market that year, accounted for 45 percent of the recalls. Foreign manufacturers were not better prepared than Detroit for the oil embargo of 1973-74; supplies of Volkswagens and Toyotas were just as tight as those of American small cars. Detroit did not arrogantly defy a continuing public demand for smaller cars after the embargo had ended, in March of 1974; by midsummer of that year, with a 60-day supply considered as normal, the industry was stuck with supplies of 96 days for the Pinto, 110 days for the Vega, 105 days for the Plymouth Valiant and 113 days for the Dodge Colt. "Few people recall today," Mr. Tucker says, "that the rebate programs of 1974 were aimed almost exclusively at clearing up backlogs of small cars." And so on, right up to the assumption that the American companies were the only ones unprepared for the most recent revival of demand for small cars: "foreign manufacturers were caught just as short-handed."

Are there no circumstances under which you would favor government intervention to save a failing industry? What about Lockheed?

Lockheed is a different case. It wasn't only that we could not afford to lose a facility because of its defense implications, or that we needed their airframe and design capabilities in weaponry. We may well need domestic competition in aircraft manufacture, as against steel and automobiles, where other nations keep the domestic companies honest.

At what point would you ask government help for your own company?

We are already asking for price protection and guaranteed contracts in connection with the production of synthetic fuels. We're asking for guaranteed loans. I ask myself what I would do if I were in charge of OPEC and I faced competition from a synfuel industry started by one of my national customers. What I would do would be to cut the price of my oil to the point where it would be uneconomical for the customer to proceed. That's why Koppers is asking for protection. We can't afford to make a huge investment that could be rendered worthless by a cartel decision.

What if OPEC does cut its prices after you've committed yourselves.

In that case, government should buy the plant and hold it in standby. Mothballing is fairly low-cost insurance against a future OPEC price rise. And this is a legitimate case for government action because it involves the interest of the entire public.

Then you do see some circumstances under which government intervention is appropriate?

I always have. There is no way we could have cleaned up our Pittsburgh air without government involvement. There is no way that we can clean up the environment or guarantee product safety or improve employee health and safety by the natural workings of a price-competitive, price-allocating system without some degree of intervention by society. Well, yes, there is. Its name is "co-operative voluntarism," and to anyone who thinks that might work, I say good luck.

Herman Kahn often tells businessmen that if they could make a profit by filling up the Grand Canyon, about half of them would do it. "The only way to protect the Grand Canyon is to protect it by law," he says, and I have to agree with him.

Can the government's role be kept within reasonable bounds?
Unfortunately, one intervention brings another, like that tangled web of deception Scott wrote about. Process engineers call it "hunting" in a system, and I like to state it as an extension of Murphy's Law: if anything can go wrong, it will, and as soon as you correct that, something else will go wrong.

We must always understand and cope with the conditions that bring politicians into power. Allan H. Meltzer, of Carnegie-Mellon's Graduate School of Industrial Administration, says:

> Government grows because there is a decisive difference between the political process and the market process. The market process distributes income according to each person's perceived contribution, as determined by the tastes, talents and opportunities that are found in society. The political process *redistributes* income according to the accepted voting norm — one person, one vote.

What do you mean when you say government should deal with the consequences of industrial failure? The picture most commonly associated with industrial failure is that of the plant town mortally stricken, people out of work, storefronts boarded up, the tax base collapsed, the community turned on its ear. Is that where government should step in?

Our first concern must be for people. A closed plant is like a burning building — we get the tenants out and attend to their needs before we turn our attention to the fire.

I'd rather talk about what *society* should do, a concept that embraces but goes beyond government.

Society should try to help workers find other employment *locally*, for minimum disruption in their lives and the lives of their families. If that proves impossible, society should seek opportunities for workers to use their skills elsewhere in the country, again with minimum disruption.

There should be a degree of protection against catastrophic health problems.

There should be reasonable continuity of earnings — at least at the sustenance level — without invasion of savings.

Where necessary, there should be job retraining. In this area, we might take a cue from the Committee for Economic Development, which has supported greater private-sector involvement in retraining and work experience through cooperation between local employers and local labor market institutions.

What should be done for the community itself?

Really, what should be done should have been undertaken long before the crisis struck. The community should be sensitive well in advance to the possible impact of change. It should think about what industry belongs there and what it has to offer to industry in terms of such factors as availability of resources, skilled labor supply and the logistics of distribution. In other words, the community should anticipate the problem instead of merely responding to it.

Are you talking about special incentives to lure industry?

What it comes down to is that it is perfectly legitimate to lure an industry on the basis of logical advantages. It is wrong, and ultimately self-defeating, to do so on the basis of bribery.

Look at what happened in Puerto Rico. Operation Bootstrap should have been used to strengthen the capital base of the area. Instead, it was used to cut prices, and the real beneficiaries were the customers outside Puerto Rico. The program did provide employment, but it was not a builder of strength of a permanent nature.

Might we preserve our industries and our communities by following the European experience in tripartite consultation among "social partners"?

I would love to see an end to the adversary relationship, but if you're talking abut a troika arrangement whereby labor, industry and government join together in dictating the course of an industry, I'm opposed to it. I'm opposed to having union representation, or any other constituency interest, on a corporate board.

I find it rather curious that some advocates are urging us to adopt such a policy at a time when the Europeans have begun the difficult task of extricating themselves from that policy, which has largely failed. It is like boarding at the bow while the crew scrambles to disembark at the stern because it knows the vessel is sinking.

Can we learn anything from the Japanese strategy of "picking the winners," providing government support for new industries that show great potential for growth?

No. Japan is virtually unique in the world. It came to the end of

World War II thoroughly devastated. It had no resources, no fuels. It had nothing to build on. Ancient civilization that it was, it arrived at 1945 with a *tabula rasa* on which it could write an entirely new strategy. Japan had to have a planned economy.

The Ministers of the Organization for Economic Co-operation and Development looked at the effort in this direction by Great Britain, whose supported industries turned up precious few winners. They concluded that this approach "is far from easy, particularly for industrial countries at the frontier of technological progress and changing patterns of consumption and possessing only roughly similar factor endowments and management skills."

How long can we go on competing in a world where others have advantages that are closed to us?

I assume you're talking about such things as wage differentials, export bias in foreign tax structure, government subsidization of commercial research and development, and unfair trade practices. We can go on complaining about these things, but there is no way that we can, or should, intervene in the policies of other sovereign nations. Unless we want to see our share of international markets for manufactured goods decline further, we will have to adapt our own industrial policy to the world as it really is.

We had better recognize, too, that not only the rules of the game, but the players, are subject to change. The tough new competition we will face in the 1980s and 1990s will come from the high-growth, newly industrializing countires, such as South Korea, Taiwan, Mexico, Brazil, Hong Kong and Singapore. They are already grabbing world market shares for products that only a decade ago were considered examples of fairly advanced technology — such things as industrial electronic components and high-quality consumer electronics, especially high-fidelity systems and television sets. Several of them are already moving into sophisticated desktop computers and are positioning themselves to hack away at our two-thirds share of the global market for high-density integrated circuits.

Would import barriers be effective against these lesser powers?

Even if such barriers made sense, we couldn't afford them. These high-growth economies are among the fastest-growing export markets for American-manufactured goods. One-fourth of all our manufactured exports now go to the developing countries.

You've been on record as calling for a stronger industrial policy. Won't this lead to more government intervention?
I haven't called for a stronger industrial policy. I've called for an industrial policy, period. We don't have one now.

Last October, the Northeast-Midwest Congressional Coalition — representing the areas that have been hit hardest by industrial failures — issued a report that called attention to our shortcomings. Although that report confined itself to import problems, it summarized one aspect of our situation in a single sentence when it said, "In no other country does trade policy exist in a vacuum, separate from domestic industrial strategies." You can extend that statement to cover our entire economy.

Yes, "industrial policy" does sound to some people like state planning, or socialism. But I am not talking about bureaucratic determination of where we should be heading. I am talking about anticipatory analysis, involving private and public leadership — both thinkers and doers — in an open and continuing process.

It is interesting that the most recent Nobel Prize in economics went to Lawrence R. Klein, of the University of Pennsylvania, whose work has focused on econometrics. I have long felt that one of our most serious handicaps is the lack of manageable data on our economy and the effect of various forces on it. For a nation that pioneered in computer technology and information retrieval, we are sadly lagging in the development of forward-looking statistical bases upon which to build our plans. We need better information, need more of it, and need to be able to get at it more expeditiously.

The *New York Times*, in a lead editorial printed in 1975, said:

The issue is no longer whether government planning would interfere with business but whether the Federal Government should act in so uncoordinated and short-sighted a way as it does now.

Efforts by government to look farther ahead and to gather, analyze and publish the information on which it is basing its policy decisions would help private industry to make its own planning decisions — without governmental coercion of the private sector. Industries would still be free to make their own investment decisions, but they would do so on the basis of more complete information about long-term trends as affected by government policies.

What would your industrial policy consist of?

More than I can tell in this short space.

It would require that we phase down our government expenditures to less than 20 percent of our gross national product.

It envisions a national investment policy that would use the tax power to help achieve priorities in the rebuilding of our infrastructure.

It would call for stricter enforcement of international trade agreements and for modifications of our antitrust policies to increase our international competitiveness.

It would entail incentives leading to the kind of investment we need for the process that has become known as "reindustrialization." We have betrayed our forebears by dissipating the capital base they handed down to us after hard work and disciplined savings. We should not cheat our posterity.

An important part of our industrial policy should be a decision not to support labor-intensive industry. We are past that point in our history, and to do so would be just as wrong as to support capital-intensive industry in those parts of the world where jobs are required for people of few skills and low levels of literacy.

I have had personal experience in this area. Some years ago, I spoke with the head of a Latin American country who wanted to build a huge petrochemical complex in a province crippled by unemployment. I tried to dissuade him. I said: "Mr. President, you will build this giant complex and you will have jobs for 3,000 people for the two and a half years required for construction and then you will have jobs for 100 people to operate it. You will have invested tremendous sums of money and in the end your problem will be no better, possibly worse."

Unfortunately, I lost that argument. And the contract.

Granted all that you have said, are things as bad as most critics paint them? After all, the great majority of Americans lead lives that are comfortable by any standard of comparison. Aren't you being a pessimist?

I'll tell you how I view the current scene, and then you can judge for yourself.

We have a growing stock of obsolete, obsolescent and uncompetitive production facilities. The average American plant today is about 20 years old, as against 12 years in Germany and 10 years in Japan. I have already talked about the trillions of dollars that will be needed to correct this situation, and I said earlier that I didn't know where the money would come from. I still don't know.

We seldom hear any more the phrase "Yankee know-how." This used to be one of our greatest sources of strength, and studies show that those companies which invest heavily in research and development enjoy a rate of productivity about two times as great as that for companies with relatively low investment in R&D. They have nine times the growth in jobs provided and their prices go up by only one-sixth as much.

Against this background, we look back on the 1970s and see that we have suffered a 10-year lag in innovation. Some figures from the Patent and Trademark Office are revealing. In 1963, 18.6 percent of U.S. patents went to foreign nationals. Fifteen years later, that share had doubled, to roughly 38 percent.

Too many companies, faced with the need to reduce the time between investment and return, feel that they cannot afford to pay for basic research to look into matters that do not promise short-term payoffs. This is unfortunate because many of our really important breakthroughs have come out of basic research. The late Charles Eames, after having built a solar-powered toy that did nothing at all — except to delight and instruct — said, "If Franklin had been looking only for a way to lift hay into the loft, he would not have discovered nearly so much about the nature of electricity."

And so forth and so on — the institutionalizing of inflation, which has acquired a constituency of its own — sluggish productivity growth — structural unemployment — declining competitiveness against foreign producers — chronic trade and payments deficits — weakening of the international value of the dollar — plummeting public confidence, at home and abroad, in the future of America's economic leadership.

It's a long list. Wouldn't you say that summary brands you a pessimist?

It depends on your definition. The great economist Joseph Schumpeter fielded a similar question when his friends accused him of being a defeatist. He wrote:

> Defeatism is a psychic state which is attributable only to the attitude with which . . .information is received. For example, the statement that a ship is sinking is not per se a defeatist statement. The attitude with which the crew re-

ceives the message may be. They may rush to drink or they may rush to man the pumps.

Me, I hope I'm a pumper and not a drinker. I compare America's present situation to that of a man swimming out to sea. If I observe such a man, I can hope that he will come across a raft, that a ship will spot him and pick him up, or that he will turn around and swim back to shore before he is exhausted. But I know that if none of these things happen, and if the man continues to swim out to sea, he will eventually drown.

How does that analogy apply to the topic of this discussion — the role of government in failing industries?

One hopes the government will provide the swimmer beforehand with a navigational chart into safe waters and will remove the dead weight with which it has encumbered him. If those things are done in time, there will be no need for an attempt at rescue.